Science Fair Success

How to Enter and Win an Invention Contest

Ed Sobey

Enslow Publishers, Inc.

40 Industrial Road PO Box 38
Box 398 Aldershot
Berkeley Heights, NJ 07922 Hants GU12 6BP
USA UK

http://www.enslow.com

To Dave Lieberth,

perpetual civic leader, producer of epic events and performances,
source of encouragement, and friend

Library of Congress Cataloging-in-Publication Data

Sobey, Edwin J. C., 1948–
    How to enter and win an invention contest / Ed Sobey.
      p. cm.—(Science fair success)
    Includes bibliographical references and index.
    Summary: Describes the history and process of invention and lists national middle
school and high school level invention contests and entrance rules, regional inventors' clubs,
and ideas for projects.
    ISBN 0-7660-1173-9
      1. Inventions—Competitions—United States—Juvenile literature. 2. Children as
inventors—United States—Juvenile literature. [1. Inventions—Competitions.]
    I. Title. II. Series.
    T339.S692   1999
    607.973—dc21   98-31753
                                               CIP
                                                 AC

Printed in the United States of America

10 9 8 7 6 5 4 3 2

To Our Readers:
All Internet addresses in this book were active and appropriate when we went to press. Any
comments or suggestions can be sent by e-mail to Comments@enslow.com or to the address on
the back cover.

Illustration Credits: © Corel Corporation, pp. 5, 8, 21, 28, 36, 43, 58, 69, 84, 94;
Shan Gordon, pp. 6, 9, 12, 15, 23, 25, 30, 33, 37, 41, 45, 50, 52, 55, 61, 65, 67, 72,
75, 80, 95, 98.

Cover Illustration: © TSM/Thom Lang, 1998 (background); Shan Gordon
(foreground).

Contents

Acknowledgments

The teachers, especially Pat Wilson, and students of Sublimity, Oregon, played a helpful role by sharing their ideas with me, and allowing photographer Shan Gordon of Positive Image Photo, Inc., to take their pictures. Thank you for your help and hospitality.

Chapter 1

Entering Invention Contests

Imagine adults asking you for your ideas on how to make something better. "We need a better transportation system. Our roads are a mess, and cars are polluting the air. What can you come up with that would replace our current system?" They need fresh ideas to solve problems. Are you ready to suggest some solutions?

Your opportunity to suggest a better way to peel potatoes, take out the trash, or get to the video store is here. Enter an invention contest. Put your creativity to the test to solve a problem.

Invention contests let you showcase your ideas. You have the chance to suggest new machines, new materials, and new ways to do things. Can you come up with a machine to sort socks, a new toy, or an accessory for a bicycle? Contest judges, the media, and the public will see your contest entry and your ideas.

What could be more fun? You brainstorm ideas, make models of the best solutions, test them, and show them off to the world. Thomas Edison, the Wright brothers, Alexander Graham Bell, and you are all members of the fraternity of inventors.

Of course, if inventing were easy to do, someone would have invented everything already. Luckily for you, there is plenty left to invent. All you need is persistence, an invention contest, and this book.

Many schools offer invention contests. If your school does not, ask your teacher, parents, and principal whether you can help get one started. The names and addresses of the largest invention contests are listed in Chapter 2.

An invention contest is a great place to share your ideas with students, judges, friends, and family.

You do not have to make your invention alone. Working with a small group of partners may give you a better invention. Gather one or two friends and decide on a challenge you want to solve. Then brainstorm together, and have fun seeing your ideas take shape.

Are ideas starting to flow through your head? Before you get too far, get a copy of the rules of the invention contest you will be entering. Make sure you follow the guidelines so your invention meets their criteria.

Show the world how inventive you can be. Crank out those ideas and enter an invention contest.

Chapter 2

National Contests You Can Enter

Invention contests challenge you to solve problems. Some contests specify one problem or one type of problem, and others let you invent anything you want. All invention contests want you to suggest new ways to do things and to demonstrate your methods with a model of your invention and a display. Inventing is not just coming up with ideas; it is making ideas work.

There are local, regional, and national invention contests. Your school can sign up to participate in an existing contest, or it can organize one itself. If your school does not offer an invention contest, you can still participate in several of the national contests listed in this chapter. So you have plenty of opportunity to enter an invention contest.

If you want to help your school organize its own invention contest (or *fair* as they are sometimes called), find a teacher who will help you coordinate the event. To get ideas for guidelines, contact national organizations and request copies of their rules. You could recruit local inventors or patent attorneys to serve as judges. You can find a listing of patent attorneys in the telephone directory (Yellow Pages, under the heading "Attorneys"). Parents may want to help, too.

Participating in one of the national contests can be easier than organizing your own contest, because the sponsors provide rules, judging criteria, and support materials. They also allow the best local inventions to go to regional, state, national, and, in some cases, international contests. Attending a statewide contest would be a fun experience. Winning one would be even more fun. Larger contests carry more prestige and sometimes big prizes, both of which are valuable to you.

Besides local inventors or patent attorneys, high school students sometimes serve as invention contest judges.

The following is a list of contests and who they are intended for. Because sponsors sometimes lose interest in organizing contests, you may find that some of these no longer exist, and others have sprung up in their place. To get the latest information, you can check out Web sites on the Internet, write to the organizations, or ask your science teachers.

Bayer/NSF Award for Community Innovation

This program, sponsored by the Bayer Corporation and the National Science Foundation, challenges teams of four students in grades six through eight to identify a community problem and invent a solution. Winning entries receive cash prizes (top prize is $20,000) and a trip to Epcot in Orlando, Florida. For information, contact Bayer/NSF at:

Bayer/NSF Award for Community Innovation
105 Terry Drive, Suite 120
Newton, PA 18940-3425
Telephone: (800) 291-6020
Fax: (215) 579-8589
E-mail: success@edumeda.com
Web site: http://www.nsf.gov/od/lpa/events/bayernsf

Craftsman/NSTA Young Inventors Awards Program

This program is sponsored by Sears, Roebuck and Company and is administered by the National Science Teachers Association (NSTA). The challenge is to invent a new tool or modify an existing tool.

The deadline is in March, and the contest is open to students in grades three through eight. The sponsors offer a variety of awards, including a top prize of a $10,000 United States savings bond. There are ten national finalists in addition to the national winner. The twelve regional winners are also awarded prizes. Winners and their parents get paid trips to the awards ceremony.

To receive an application and rules, contact the NSTA at:

Craftsman/NSTA Young Inventors Awards Program
National Science Teachers Association
1840 Wilson Boulevard
Arlington, VA 22201-3000
Telephone: (888) 494-4994
E-mail: younginventors@nsta.org
Web site: http://www.nsta.org/programs/craftsman.htm

Duracell/NSTA Scholarship Competition

The NSTA conducts another invention contest every year. The contest is funded by Duracell, the battery company. You can probably find a science teacher at your school who is a member of the NSTA and has current information on the contest.

This competition is open to all United States students in grades six through twelve. You can enter as an individual or as a team of two students. To enter, you need to design and build a machine powered by Duracell batteries. You will complete an entry form, write a two-page description of the device and how it can be used, draw a wiring diagram of the electric circuits you designed, and send a photograph of the device.

If your entry is one of the top one hundred (out of about eight hundred inventions entered each year), the NSTA will ask you to mail in the device you invented.

Written entries are due by mid-January. If teachers attend one of the NSTA conferences (there are several regional conferences and one national conference every year), they can sign up to get a starter kit of information that includes electronic supplies.

If none of your teachers has the information, you can get the official entry form by calling the NSTA at (888) 255-4242.

The awards are substantial. First-place prize is a $20,000 United States savings bond. They award about one hundred prizes. Teachers of students winning top awards also get awards.

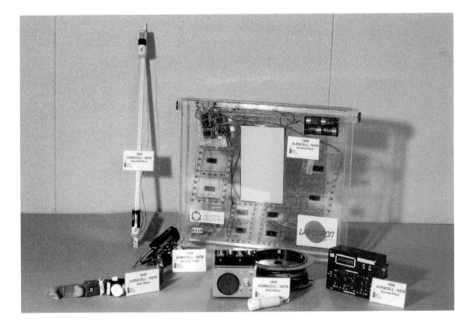

The annual Duracell/NSTA Scholarship Competition requires contestants to design and build a machine powered by Duracell batteries. The winning 1998 entries are pictured here.

To get more information, contact the NSTA at:

Duracell/NSTA Scholarship Competition
National Science Teachers Association
1840 Wilson Boulevard
Arlington, VA 22201-3000
Telephone: (888) 255-4242
Fax: (703) 243-7177
E-mail: duracell@nsta.org
Web site: http://www.nsta.org/programs/duracell.htm

Invent America!

This is one of the most recognized names among invention contests. Unfortunately, the organization sponsoring the contest has had difficulties in recent years. Check with their offices to see when they will be offering their next contest.

Their program is open to all United States students from kindergarten through eighth grade. To enroll, your school has to purchase an enrollment kit. Individual families can enter by buying a family kit. Check with their home page to get current pricing.

You can contact Invent America! at:

Invent America!
P.O. Box 26065
Alexandria, VA 22313
Telephone: (703) 684-1836
Web site: http://www.inventamerica.org

Invent the Future

Intel Corporation, maker of computer chips, sponsors this contest to "encourage creativity and innovation, as well as strengthening students' math and science skills." It is open to students in grades five through nine; however, Intel only offers it to students in select cities (Houston, Texas; Kansas City, Missouri; Los Angeles, California; New York, New York; Portland, Oregon; Providence, Rhode Island; Saint Paul, Minnesota; San Jose, California; and Scottsdale, Arizona). In the future they may open the contest to students in other cities. The challenge is to invent something that will "improve the future." For more information, you can visit them on the Internet at:

Web site: http://www.intel.com/intel/smithso/invent/intro.htm

Invention and Design Contest

This annual event is sponsored by LeTourneau University in Longview, Texas. It is open to all elementary and middle school students. They have separate divisions for grades two and three, grade four, grade five, and grades six through eight. They award cash prizes (ranging from $10 to $100) and have more than three hundred entries on display.

Entries must be accompanied by an entry form and must have a working prototype. A prototype is a final model of your invention. Also, you must set up a display with your invention at LeTourneau University.

"Bicycle Blinkers" won top honors in 1998. It is a safety light for bicyclists that warns others whenever the brakes are applied.

For more information, contact:

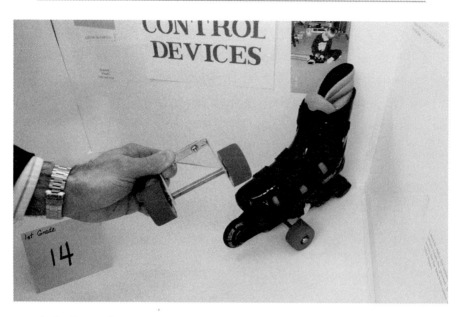

A display with a prototype, like the one pictured here, is required for LeTourneau University's Invention and Design Contest.

LeTourneau University
Office of University Relations
P.O. Box 7001
Longview, TX 75607
Telephone: (903) 233-3672
Fax: (903) 233-3618
Web site: http://www.letu.edu/community/invention

Invention Convention

Sponsored by the schoolbook publisher Silver Burdett Ginn, the Invention Convention is one of the most well-recognized invention contests. The goal is "to encourage students to apply basic science skills in a creative and productive manner." The sponsors have laid out a process to follow in preparing entries for the Annual International Invention Convention, and they conduct a national competition. You may submit your school's

Invention Convention entries online. Each school may submit only one entry for grades one through three and one entry for grades four through six. You can contact them at:

Silver Burdett Ginn Science
Annual International Invention Convention
299 Jefferson Road
Parsippany, NJ 07054-0480
Telephone: (800) 848-9500, ext. 382
Web site: http://www.sbgschool.com/teacher_activities/
convention/index.html

National Engineering Design Challenge (NEDC)

This annual competition for high school students (grades nine through twelve) is organized by the Junior Engineering Technical Society (JETS). The JETS defines one problem each year for teams around the country to solve. At regional, state, and national levels, teams of students demonstrate their solutions to panels of experts. The problem for 1997–98 was to redesign the shopping cart such that it reduces "the possibility that a two-year-old child will fall out or climb out of it and that it resists tipping when a child leans over the edge."

You can get more information on the NEDC by contacting the JETS at:

Junior Engineering Technical Society
1420 King Street, Suite 405
Alexandria, VA 22314-2794
Telephone: (703) 548-5387
Fax: (703) 548-0769
E-mail: jets@nae.edu
Web site: http://www.asee.org/jets/nedc/nedc.html

National Gallery for America's Young Inventors

This unique program honors inventions created by young inventors. Each year it inducts up to six inventors from kindergarten through twelfth grade. Their program coincides with the annual induction into the National Inventors Hall of Fame, which is located only two hundred yards away. The National Gallery is run by a nonprofit organization, Partnership for America's Future, Inc. You can get information by contacting:

Partnership for America's Future, Inc.
80 West Bowery Street, Suite 305
Akron, OH 44308
Telephone: (330) 376-8300
E-mail: PAFINC@akronet.com

National Toy Hall of Fame

The National Toy Hall of Fame opened in 1998 at the A. C. Gilbert's Discovery Village in Salem, Oregon, to honor the great toys that shape the lives of people growing up and to encourage young people to invent their own toys. Annually they select a small number of kid-invented toys to display alongside the toys inducted into the Hall of Fame. To be considered, send a written description and a photo or illustration of a toy you have invented to:

A. C. Gilbert's Discovery Village
116 Marion Street, NE
Salem, OR 97301-3437
Telephone: (800) 208-9514
Fax: (503) 316-3485
E-mail: info@acgilbert.org
Web site: http://www.acgilbert.org

Science Olympiad

Science Olympiad has competitions for elementary, middle, and high school teams in which students demonstrate their knowledge of science or solve specific engineering and science problems. Several of the events require inventing skills. For more information, check with science teachers at your school or check out the Science Olympiad Web page.

Science Olympiad
5955 Little Pine Lane
Rochester, MI 48306
Telephone: (810) 651-4013
Fax: (810) 651-7835
Web site: http://www.geocities.com/CapeCanaveral/Lab/9699

Sea World/Busch Gardens Environmental Excellence Awards

This contest recognizes student groups working to "protect and preserve the environment." Although this contest is not specifically geared to inventions, you could submit an invention that meets the goals. They offer $100,000 in prizes.

Applications are due in late February. To get an application, contact:

Sea World/Busch Gardens Environmental Excellence Awards
Education Department
7007 Sea World Drive
Orlando, FL 32821
Telephone: (407) 363-2389
Web site: http://www.seaworld.com/seaworld/sw_florida/
swfframe.html; then choose "Environmental News."

Toshiba/NSTA ExploraVision Awards

Funded by Toshiba and also organized by the National Science Teachers Association, the ExploraVision Awards encourage future-thinking. To participate, organize a team of three or four students to "envision technologies that could exist twenty years in the future." A technology could be computers, elevators, or television. The competition is open to United States and Canadian students.

You conduct research on the technology, brainstorm its future, and create a storyboard that shows your ideas. If you win at the regional level of the competition, you get to make a video about your ideas to present at the national competition.

Teams compete in four divisions: Primary (kindergarten to third grade), Upper Elementary (grades four to six), Middle Level (grades seven to nine), and High School (grades ten to twelve). Cash prizes are given and some teams win Toshiba computing equipment for their schools. Entries selected at the regional level each receive $100 savings bonds, and their schools receive a Toshiba television and videocassette recorder (VCR). Members of the eight second-place teams at the national competition each receive $5,000 savings bonds. Four teams (one from each grade division) win first-place prizes of a $10,000 savings bond for each team member. Students of the top twelve teams and their parents will travel to Washington, D.C., to receive their prizes.

A recent winning entry in the Primary division was called "Kid Watch." The team suggested that young people could not get lost if they wore a microcomputer linked to orbiting satellites to keep track of them.

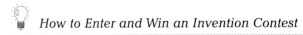

For more information, contact the NSTA at:

Toshiba/NSTA ExploraVision Awards

National Science Teachers Association

1840 Wilson Boulevard

Arlington, VA 22201-3000

Telephone: (800) EXPLOR-9

Fax: (703) 243-7177

E-mail: exploravision@nsta.org

Web site: http://www.toshiba.com/tai/exploravision/index3.htm

Chapter 3

Becoming an Inventor

Aside from the famous inventors of the lightbulb, telephone, and airplane, can you name another inventor? Inventors are people who create new processes, machines, or objects, or who modify these things in new ways. You may already have invented a new game or toy or a tool to help you do a job. If you did, you are an inventor.

Everyone has ideas, but few people turn their ideas into useful products. Only inventors do that. And, although everyone has abilities to create something new, only inventors persevere to make their ideas work.

Traits of Inventors

If everyone can invent, why are so few people inventors? Many people may have an invention idea for an improvement or new product, but they do not do anything with their idea. They want someone else to make it work and sell it. Inventors take creative ideas, usually their own, and transform them into products that people can buy and use. They turn their ideas into models and are persistent enough to keep working on an invention when others may have given up.

A special trait of inventors is that they ask lots of questions. Inventors are learners. They have boundless curiosity. They are constantly seeking answers to questions and constantly asking more questions. They never know enough. Inventors think a lot about technical problems and how to solve them, and they often think with their hands as well as their minds. The only way to know how something will work is to build a model and try it, so inventors build and experiment—they tinker. And they keep tinkering long after most people would have quit.

These are the traits of inventors, and if you want to invent something, you should be just as curious, hardworking, and persistent as other inventors. Who are the great inventors? Here are just a few.

The Great Inventors

The great inventors are women and men from all ethnic backgrounds who have solved the troublesome problems of their era. Some, like Alexander Graham Bell, who invented the telephone, made fortunes. Others, like Charles Goodyear, who invented the process of vulcanization (making rubber a useful material), died with no money. Some were great scientists and Nobel Prize winners, like Gertrude Belle Elion, who discovered several drugs to fight leukemia and other diseases. Many, like Herman Hollerith, who invented the first electric

No need to fuss with a slippery bar of soap in the shower. Just turn the knob and soap mixes with water as it flows through the shower head. Inventors take creative ideas like this and turn them into useful products.

tabulating machines, prospered working alone; and some, like Stephanie Kwolek, who invented Kevlar, worked for major corporations. (Kevlar is a heat- and chemical-resistant fiber sold by the Du Pont Company. It is used in many products, including bulletproof vests, rope, skis, and tires.)

Many inventors started their own companies to manufacture the products they invented. William Hewlett invented the audio oscillator and, with David Packard, started the giant electronics company Hewlett-Packard. The first practical car radio was made by William Lear, who started the Motorola Company and later invented Learjets. Digital Equipment Corporation (DEC) was started by Ken Olsen, who contributed to the development of the magnetic core memory for computers. The steam brake launched George Westinghouse on his career as an inventor and founder of the Westinghouse Corporation. John Deere improved the plow and started a company that today makes lawn mowers and earth-moving equipment. Arriving in the United States from his native home in China with very little money, An Wang invented computer components and formed the Wang Laboratories. A. C. Gilbert held more than one hundred fifty patents. He invented Erector Set construction toys and many other toys, all of which were produced by his A. C. Gilbert Company.

Common to all inventors is their ability to overcome problems. Percy Julian had to live in Europe because, as an African American, he could not get an advanced education in the United States. He received his doctorate degree in Austria and returned home to create synthetic drugs, including cortisone and paint chemicals. Later he served on the board of trustees

Persistence, curiosity, and hard work enabled this student to build his invention. The invention is a remote-control car with the wheels replaced by a hair dryer that elevates the car above the floor.

for one of the colleges that had refused to admit him as a student.

Chester Carlson invented a process that has become vital to nearly every business and school in America. He invented electrophotography, or photocopying. As important as the process is today, he spent nine years trying to find a company to make and sell copy machines. Most of the major companies did not see the value in being able to make copies of documents. Today those same companies own and use many copy machines.

Great inventors come up with ideas on how to improve things, and they work hard to turn their ideas into useful products. You can do that!

If the stories of great inventors interest you, check out the holdings of your library or go to the Web site of the National Inventors Hall of Fame at <http://www.invent.org>.

How You Can Become an Inventor

To be a great inventor, think and work like one. Ask lots of questions, learn all you can, be open to new ideas, build and test models of your ideas, and do not give up.

Find one or two areas that interest you, and learn everything you can about them. Ask the experts, the people who work in that area, what their little problems are. Someone is probably already working on the big problems, so you should focus on the small ones. When you come up with an idea to solve the problem, build the device and test it. Inventing is not only coming up with ideas; it is finding solutions to problems and making those solutions work.

Know what you want to do, and do not give up. If Thomas Edison had given up after the first hundred or two hundred or even one thousand attempts to invent the lightbulb, he would have failed. It took him nearly two thousand tries to invent a long-lived lightbulb. Edison did not quit, and neither should you.

Chapter 4

How to Get Started

Once you have decided what invention contest you would like to enter, request a copy of the guidelines so you can get an early start. Remember, if your school does not have an invention contest, get the guidelines for entering one or more of the national contests.

Study the guidelines for the contest you want to enter, and make sure you understand what criteria the judges will use to evaluate inventions. Remind yourself of what those criteria are while you are inventing. Also, mark a calendar with all the dates of the contest. You do not want to be so busy that you forget to submit your entry form on time.

Are you ready to invent a new widget? Not many people suddenly wake up in the morning with a great idea for an invention. Most ideas arise when inventors have been working on a problem and thinking about it for a while. To help themselves come up with new ideas, successful inventors have systems for preparing their minds. Here are some steps you can follow that will direct you during your journey to the invention contest.

Step 1: Start Your Inventor's Log

Start a notebook of problems and ideas—an inventor's log. An inexpensive bound notebook is best. Once you have the notebook, start filling it up. Get in the habit of recording all the problems you encounter throughout the day. When you write them in the log, add a note on what a solution might do or might be.

For example, let's say the problem you saw was that your book bag falls off your shoulder when you use only one strap. You would make an entry in your notebook stating the problem and the date. Even if you do not know what the solution to the problem is, write what the solution might do. One solution could be making the strap stick to your shoulder. By writing what the solution might do, you alert your brain to start looking for ways to make that happen. In this case, you might think of using Velcro strips or a hook and eye to keep the strap from slipping.

Other things to record in your log are sources for materials, important dates for the invention contest, phone numbers of people who can help you, books you use, and sketches of ideas and inventions. It is handy to keep all your inventing information in one place.

When you make mock-ups or models of your invention (see Step 6), you can use your log to record how long they took to make, what materials you used, and ideas for making them better. You can also record data from testing your invention (Step 7).

These students improved a situation in their home by adapting chemical hand warmers into the covered seat of a toilet to provide a warmer surface.

If you get in the habit of recording all the information about your invention in your inventor's log, you will always know where to find it. Some invention contests want you to display your inventor's log along with your invention.

Your log also documents that you have done all the work yourself and the dates when you did it, information that is important for protecting your ideas. In legal battles to decide which inventor should receive a patent, courts look at inventor's logs to see who first had the idea. The invention of the laser provides a good example.

Charles Townes was awarded the patent for the laser and received royalties for years. However, Gordon Gould was later able to show that he had the idea before Townes. Gould's inventor's log had a written description of a laser, a diagram of how it might work, and the word *laser* at an earlier date than Townes could show. So years after the Patent Office awarded the patent to Townes, the courts took it away from him and awarded it to Gould. Make sure you keep a record of all your ideas and the dates you had them.

Step 2: Find Problems to Solve

The next thing you need to do when you are considering entering an invention contest is to find problems to solve. Then you can start to think of ways to solve them. Or you may also begin to devise ways to improve upon an existing product. Begin to think, "How can I invent something to do a better job?"

There are countless problems to find, some of which you can solve, and many you cannot. You may not be able to invent a new type of computer game, but you could invent a carrying case to carry game cartridges.

Even the tough problems are worth remembering because tomorrow you might find the perfect solution for one of them. The more problems you recognize and remember, the more likely you are to solve one of them.

As you are thinking about the problems, ask other people about them. They may have some ideas on solutions, or they may suggest other problems for you to solve. Inventors collect problems like some people collect baseball cards.

How to Find Problems

We are always looking for faster computers, more fuel-efficient cars, and more powerful rockets. But, unless you are a computer engineer, automobile designer, or rocket scientist, you may not be able to solve these problems. Of course, if you study hard you could become a computer engineer, automobile designer, or rocket scientist.

Rocket scientists are able to improve rockets because they understand how rockets work. Just as they are the experts on rockets, you are the expert on the things you do every day. For example, who knows how to do your chores at home better than you? Who knows the challenges young people face every day? So look for problems to solve in your daily activities.

What do you do? Do you have hobbies? Do you play sports or games? Do you collect things? If you collect things, how do you show them to others? Is it easy or hard? How do you keep them clean and out of the way when you are not showing them? For sports and games, is it a problem finding the equipment you need? If you find the bat, will you find the ball nearby?

Do you have chores or jobs that you have to do? Are there some you wish you did not have to do? Taking out the garbage and cleaning up after pets are not always fun chores. Raking leaves may rank pretty high on the boring index, too. Could you invent a device that would make these jobs easier, faster, or more fun? Since you know these jobs well, you are the best person to invent an improvement.

Take your inventor's attitude with you throughout the day as you do your hobbies and chores. Keep asking yourself whether it might be possible to invent something that would make the chores easier or the hobbies more fun. Even if you do not know how to solve the problems, keep a record of your

To make a basketball game more challenging, two students invented a device that straps onto the rim, decreasing the size of the opening and making it tougher to sink a shot.

ideas in your inventor's log so you can think about them later. Then let your brain work awhile on finding a solution.

If you have trouble finding problems to solve, ask others. Take a survey of the types of inventions people would most like to have. Ask them to name a few of the small annoying problems that bug them at work, at school, at home, in the car, in the yard, or at play. Many of their ideas might require inventions that no one could invent, but someone might give you the perfect idea. Talking to people about inventing may also lead you to discover some problem you have never thought about before. So grab your inventor's log and pencil, and start your survey.

Step 3: Pick One Problem

You may be working on finding solutions for many problems, but you have to focus on just one problem to solve for your invention contest. You cannot tell the judges that you have so many problems to work on that you did not have time to solve one.

Which problem do you pick? *It is best to choose a problem that is both fun to solve and solvable.* If it is not fun, you will lose interest. Inventing is fun, and picking the right problem makes it more fun. Of course, picking a problem you cannot solve means you will not have a solution to show the judges. Unlike science fairs, where grand failures to prove hypotheses are just as valuable as grand successes, in invention contests you need to demonstrate that you have successfully created something new that solves a problem. When you start working on a problem, you may not know what the solution is, but you should be able to guess whether or not you can find it. Ending world hunger will probably elude your most valiant efforts, but making a gizmo to remove jar lids might not. No matter how noble the former is, the latter is doable, and you need a doable project.

Check the criteria your particular invention contest uses to select the winning entries. The judging criteria can steer you to picking a problem. Judges may be interested in seeing a working model, or they may not care as much about the model but be more interested in your presentation board. Find out what they want before you start working on a project that may not fit their criteria.

The following chapters (5–7) will help you while you are choosing one idea for an invention contest. There are many different ways to invent, as you will see in Chapter 5. Chapters 6 and 7 give examples of things you can invent, whether they be for the home, school, or car.

When you have decided what you would like to invent, continue with Steps 4–9 in Chapter 8 to build and present your invention for the contest.

Chapter 5

Different Ways to Invent

As you are choosing an idea for your invention contest, it is important to think about the different ways of inventing solutions. There is not just one technique used in inventing, but several different approaches that can help you invent a solution to a problem.

Considering Types of Solutions

You may imagine that inventors sit back in their chairs and think up new ideas. Actually, most inventions are adaptations of things that others have done before. Even the great inventions, like the lightbulb and airplane, were improvements on earlier attempts. So your great invention does not have to be an entirely new idea. It could be any of several things:

1. An improvement. Next time you go to a hardware store, check out all the tools. A big hardware store may carry dozens of models of hammers, dozens more of screwdrivers and wrenches, and many kinds of fasteners including nails, tacks, screws, and bolts. Each different shape was invented by someone who had an idea of how to improve the existing models. What is neat about inventing improvements is knowing that people already use the item and will likely want the new, improved version.

2. A combination. Can you take two existing products and combine them to make something new? Like what? Someone took a clock and a radio and combined them into a clock radio. A telephone and a tape recorder were combined to make an answering machine. You could start by listing all the tools and products you can think of. Then randomly pick two and see what new machine you can design. This would be a fun game for you and your friends to try.

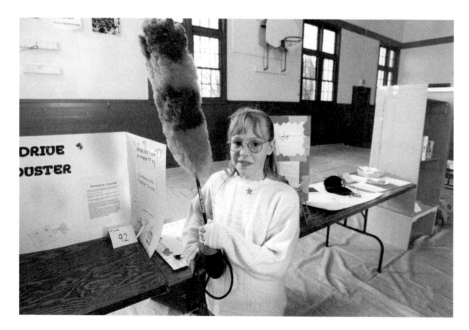

This student combined a duster and an electric drill into a "Drive Duster" that gets cobwebs out of the corners of ceilings and other places.

3. A technology loan. Find out how someone solved a similar problem and use their solution for the problem you are solving. Zippers, for example, were first used as fasteners on boots. Later, clothing designers borrowed the solution and used them in clothes. There is no need to come up with a new technology if you can just borrow an existing one.

4. Something new. These are the hardest to imagine, but once in a while you may have a great, new idea.

Breaking Mountains into Molehills

It is easier to solve small problems than big ones, so break down your problem into the smallest pieces you can.

You might draw a brain diagram of the problem, showing all the pieces. A brain diagram shows the relationship of the parts of a problem in a way that makes it easier to think about them. The diagram mimics the way your brain thinks. Start by thinking of one or two words that describe your problem, and write them within a circle in the center of a sheet of paper. Then, think of each component, or aspect, of the problem and write each in a different area surrounding the one- or two-word description. Draw lines to show connections between each component and related components, and between each component and the description. Then try to break down each component even further. Figure 1 shows an example (taking out the trash) of both problems (circles) and some potential solutions (rectangles).

To solve your big problem, you might only have to solve one of the tiny problems. For example, if the worst thing about taking out the trash is the smell, you could make the job more pleasant by spraying an air freshener into the can.

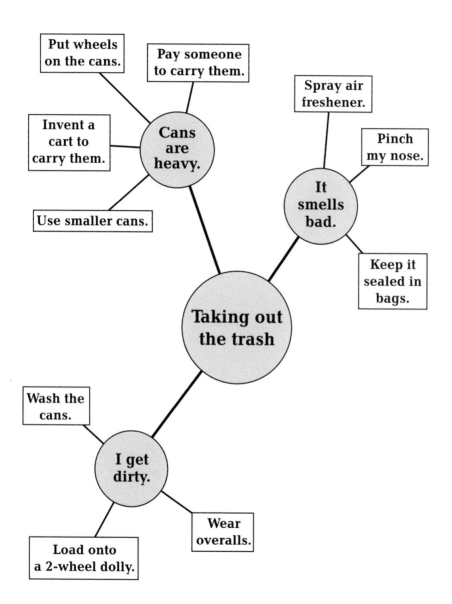

Figure 1. A brain diagram can be drawn to help you find new ways to solve a problem.

Maybe you could invent a device that attaches to the lid and releases the air freshener.

If you are trying to improve an existing invention, start by listing all the qualities or attributes of that invention: For example, what materials it is made of; how big it is; what its source of power is; what waste it produces; how easy it is to use. Focus on each of the attributes and try changing one or two of them to make an improvement.

Jump-Starting Ideas

Here are several ways to help you find ideas for solutions. Remember: When you get an idea for a solution, even if you think it might not work, write it in your inventor's log. Later, when you look at your notebook, your notes may help you come up with an even better idea.

1. Tell someone else. To describe a problem to someone, you have to think through the problem in great detail. So describing it to someone else may help you understand it better. Also, the other person may have a fresh idea on how to solve it.

2. Write about it. Another way to think about a problem is to write about it. Find the words to describe the problem and potential solutions, and write them in your inventor's log.

3. Make a drawing. Making a sketch and looking at it may trigger new ideas for solutions. Just as talking or writing about a problem helps you think about it, so too does drawing. As you draw it, you have to put in more and different details than you thought of before drawing it. These details may help you find a solution. Telling, writing, and drawing use different mental abilities, and you want to use them all to understand your problem and figure out solutions.

This combination portable radio with earphones and built-in light solved the problem of listening to music while walking outside at night.

4. Envision solutions. Focus on the solution instead of the problem. What will a solution do? If you can imagine the good things that a solution will achieve, that vision may help you see the solution itself.

5. Think of the opposite. Imagine the opposite of the real problem you are trying to solve. For example, let's say your real problem is how to keep your book-bag strap from slipping off your shoulder. Play with the opposite idea—that your problem is how to make it slide off your shoulder. To make it slide off your shoulder, you could make the strap out of a slippery material or out of rope so that it rolls off. That might give you an idea to solve your real problem—design a strap with materials that grip and are wide so it will not roll. By solving the reverse problem, you can often find a solution to the original problem.

6. Make it bigger or smaller. Could you solve the problem if it were ten times bigger or one tenth the size? Sometimes changing the size of the problem leads to seeing a solution.

7. Move it. Would it be easy to solve if the problem were in outer space or at the North Pole? Where would you have to go to make your problem easier to solve?

8. Brainstorm. Gather a group of friends to help you solve the problem. Ask them to come up with as many solutions as they can in just a few minutes. The rules for brainstorming are simple: You record all of the ideas, and no one criticizes any of them. Everyone has to listen to the ideas that others suggest, and anyone can try to expand or change them to make them better. Out of the many ideas, you are bound to find a few good ones.

9. Sleep on it. Great solutions often arise when your brain has had some quality time to itself. Define the problem and think about it in terms of what a solution might do, then put your brain on autopilot. In the morning, at breakfast or in the shower, a solution may appear out of nowhere.

Keeping a Record

Remember to record the solutions you come up with in your inventor's log. You will not use most of them now, but you might use some later. Your good ideas are very important and you do not want to forget them!

Chapter 6

Things You Can Invent

By this time you may have a long list of ideas for things you could improve or invent. If not, be sure to start a list today. In this chapter some needed inventions are presented. You can use any of these ideas to make an invention, or you can think about the ideas to see whether they inspire you to come up with different ones.

The inventions are organized in five categories: projects at school, around the house, and at the store (Chapter 6); projects in your car, and toys and games (Chapter 7). Since you spend most of your time at home and school, these are two places to look for invention ideas. Of course, if you have hobbies or experience in other fields, you might also look there for invention ideas.

As you read through the description of invention needs, be sure to write your ideas in your inventor's log.

Projects at School

Mail pouch. Have you ever had the problem of not getting important papers from school to home? Even if you have not, lots of other students have. There are notes from the parents' organization about the bake sale or magazine sale, notes about field trips, and lost-and-found notices. Too often these papers never arrive home from school, or they arrive the morning after the event. How could you improve the flow of information between school and home?

Diplomats carry special briefcases to hold important papers as they travel from capital to capital around the world. Maybe you could invent a special mail pouch or case so the papers would not get crushed in the bottom of book bags, or a wristband that contains the information; students could wear it until their parents remove it at home. Can you think of a better approach?

Bike racks. How do you get to school? In nice weather do you ride your bike? Many schools have bike racks so you can store your bike safely and neatly. But do the bike racks do everything they could?

Check out the problems people have using bike racks. If you are the last to get to school, it can be tough squeezing your bike into the sea of wheels to get it close to the rack. And if you do, can you get your lock on it securely? Have you ever heard of a bike being stolen from the rack? Or someone forgetting to bring their lock? Or losing the key or forgetting the combination?

Pick any one of these problems and solve it to make a better bike rack. Think how many schools there are and how

Some inventions make life easier, like this holder that keeps sunglasses handy, yet safe.

many bike racks each one has. The number of sales for your invention could be in the tens of thousands.

Chalkboard erasers. Some schools use the old chalkboards or blackboards, but many new schools use "white boards" with dry eraser pens. Each type of board has to be cleaned, and each one can be messy.

One of the reasons fewer schools use chalkboards is that the dust from the chalk is messy. After a few erasings, the erasers are full of chalk dust and someone has to bang them together outside to get rid of the dust. What a mess! Then, once a week or so, someone has to wash the board to get it really clean. There must be a better way.

Dry erase boards seem to be a better solution, but the erasers do not clean the boards completely. These boards need to be washed with a special fluid to get rid of the dark marks.

Whichever type of boards your school uses, see if you can figure out a more efficient way to clean them.

Automatic aquarium feeder. Some classrooms have cages and aquariums with animals that need feeding. Who feeds them when everyone is on vacation or at home during the weekends? Can you devise a machine that will give them the right amount of food?

For animals that need water, can you make a system that will ensure they get what they need? Of course, you cannot rely on an untested system to supply water; make sure it works before using it during vacations.

Automatic attendance taker. Everyone is concerned with the quality of education you and your friends are getting. One way to improve learning is for teachers to spend more time teaching and less time doing administrative chores, like taking attendance.

Check out how much time teachers use every day by taking attendance. If you asked a teacher, he or she would say that it is necessary to take roll. If they did not check attendance, some students would skip classes. To some people, that would sound convincing, but to an inventor, that would sound like an invitation to find a better way.

Why does the teacher have to call roll? Why not have a machine do it automatically? At the grocery store, does the clerk call roll?: "Peas—yup, they're here, and they cost forty-nine cents a pound." No! The clerk passes the packaged food over a scanning laser that reads the bar code on the package. The computer looks up the price and adds it to the bill automatically.

What if every student had a student identification card? Many schools have them already. One side could have the picture and name, and the other side could have a bar code to identify the student. As students walk into the classroom, a scanner reads their bar code, checks them off the list, and sends the information to the school office.

Undoubtedly you can think of reasons that such a system might not work. But an inventor anticipates such problems and works through them to make the invention work.

With a personal computer and other equipment, you could demonstrate such a system. Or maybe you could come up with a better system. Your invention could make our education system better without lengthening the time spent at school.

Getting a grip on basketballs. Have you ever watched the equipment manager at a basketball game? He or she has to pick up many basketballs and get them on and off the court for practice. How do you catch, move, and store large spherical objects?

Would it be easier to build a ramp that lets the balls roll back into the equipment room? Or could you devise a giant box the manager could raise and lower from the underside of the roof? Maybe you could make a ball catapult: A strong stream of air or a string could loft the balls into a basket at the end of the court where they could roll into the equipment room. Or maybe it would be easier to deflate the balls and carry them off. Of course, you would then need to invent a quick-inflation system so the balls would be ready when the players needed them.

Games for learning. People can learn lots of things when they have fun learning. Can you create a game or toy that is fun to play and helps people learn? It could be a mathematics-based game. For example, students could race each other or the clock to solve arithmetic problems. Or maybe you could make a game board that shows the states of the United States or the countries of the world and has question-and-answer cards about geography. Get three answers correct and win a vacation to Hawaii—at least on the game board.

When people compete with friends in games, they have fun. So try making a competition in which they compete while recalling some information or figuring something out.

Around the House

Mail delivery. Has the letter carrier come already? If your mail is delivered to a mailbox along the street, how do you know when the postal carrier has delivered the mail? Do you have to walk to the box to find out? If you are waiting for something really important or fun in the mail, you might make several trips before the carrier delivers. Or worse, you might miss the delivery and still be waiting inside when the package or letter is sitting in the mailbox.

How could you know if there is mail in the box? You could invent an electric switch that turns on a light when there is mail inside. Or you could create something to indicate that the mailbox door has been moved since the last time you reset the indicator. See what you can come up with. Maybe the mail carrier has some ideas.

Staying cool. In the middle of summer you need a way to stay cool. In what ways could you cool yourself when you are outside?

You could let water evaporate from a wet cloth you wear on your head or neck. Or you could make a battery-powered fan that you attach to your hat. A different approach would be to shade yourself from the sun so you do not heat up as much; you could make a sun-umbrella that straps to a backpack so you could keep your hands free. How about making clothing that has waterproof bags for pockets where you could store ice cubes? What other ways could you invent to keep yourself cool?

The Midas touch. What do you do with coins? Do you spend them, or do you collect them in a large jar? If you or someone at home collects them, you may dread the job of having to sort, count, and roll them. It could take hours if you have a huge pile.

Banks use expensive machines to do this work. Could you invent some simple machines to do this at home? First, you need a machine to sort the coins. You could sort by size:

This invention lets you know when the newspaper has arrived. When the paper is slid into the box, it pushes on a lever that raises a flag.

Dimes are smaller, nickels are slightly larger, and quarters are much larger. Your sorter should let you quickly separate different coins into their own piles.

Next you need to count them. Of course, you do not want to count fifty pennies each time to fill a roll. You could make a measuring device, fifty pennies long, to measure the pennies without having to count them each time. Or you could "count" them by weighing them. When you get a pile of fifty pennies, a scale tips to indicate you have enough.

Finally, you need some way of holding them so you can slide a paper wrapper or roller around them. You can get the wrappers from a bank, so you can experiment with different sizes and shapes of devices to hold the coins.

Do not let the weeds win. If you live in a house that has a yard, you probably have some chores for maintaining the yard. Can you figure out an easier way to rake leaves or grass clippings? Once you rake them into a pile, how do you get them into a container? Can you come up with an easier way?

Weeding a garden can be tough work. What type of machine would make it easier? Can you make a tool that would let you weed the garden while standing instead of having to kneel?

The next time you go into a hardware or garden store, check out the variety of tools they sell. See how many different sizes and shapes of shovels they have. Look at all the other tools and remember that people are inventing new ones each year. You could be, too.

Sports haulers. Many sports require you to carry bulky or heavy equipment. Think of scuba divers lugging tanks, weight belts, fins, masks, and other gear. Bowlers may carry

Here is an improvement on the umbrella—it keeps your hands free!

their own ball, glove, and shoes. Skiers have long skis and poles, plus heavy boots. Can you make it easier for people to carry their sports equipment?

Computer holdups. Computer users need tables or desks to hold up their computers. Can you design and build a more effective one?

Consider the ideal height of the table and the dimensions of the top. Do you want it to hold the printer and monitor? Should it have a built-in mouse pad? Maybe you should make a really big one so the mouse does not run off the edges all the time. Where and how do you store the software and disks? Is there a space for an external hard drive, scanner, or fax machine? Where do you put paper and other supplies for the printer?

Think of the difficulties you encounter when using a computer and see if you can design a computer desk that will eliminate some of the problems.

Lunch box. Do you take your lunch, or buy it at school? If you take it, what do you carry it in? Do you use a brown paper bag and squish things around? Or do you have a funky, hard-shelled box? Or maybe a soft-sided container? How could you improve any of these?

Do you ever order a pizza or go out to pick up food for dinner? What types of containers does that food come in? Do the containers work well? Do they keep hot food hot and cold stuff, like ice cream, really cold? Could you make a better way to insulate food for its trip to your house? Should you add a liquid-crystal strip thermometer to show the temperature of the food inside? If the pizza has cooled, should the restaurant give it to you for free?

If you cannot think of a way to improve the way you carry your food, can you make the container more fun? What would you put on the outside of a lunch box to make it a "must-have" item for everyone at your school? Would you build a tiny radio receiver on the outside? A walkie-talkie so you could talk to friends across the cafeteria? A computer game? Or maybe a computer pet to eat your virtual leftovers.

Tool time. Where do you think you would find the greatest variety of tools at home? A good guess would be in the kitchen. Check out how many different knives, choppers, scrapers, scissors, pots, pans, scoops, pot holders, and ice cream scoops you have. And more are invented every year.

Talk to the kitchen-gadget experts in your family. Ask them what the problems are. They might say getting lids off jars, cleaning the inside of narrow bottles and glasses, chopping up stuff, keeping grease from splattering everywhere, keeping countertops clean and clear, or keeping the lid on the cookie jar are their problems.

Once you find some problems, brainstorm some solutions. Maybe your kitchen invention could even be advertised on cable television.

Tool shed. Garden tools, shop tools, and kitchen utensils all have something in common. Without a good storage system, they tend to clutter up the work area. Check around your house and school to find where tools are tossed into a drawer or into the corner of a closet or shed. Would a tool container or hanging system make them easier to find and reduce the mess?

What kind of rack or container would be the most effective? Should it be versatile so it can handle many different tools? Or should it be specialized to hold a few tools very well?

Recycling. Do you have to haul out the trash or recyclables every week? How could you make that job easier? Could you invent a cart to carry out all the containers? It could hold the containers during the week to make it easier for you to drop stuff in, while it saves floor space in your garage. On trash night, you could wheel the entire apparatus out to the curb, ready for morning pickup.

Does your recycling container ever overflow? If everything were crushed, you would probably have enough room. So how do you crush tin cans and milk cartons? Can you make a simple device to crush the common containers that get recycled?

Electronic turn-ons. Microsoft chairman Bill Gates built a mansion near his office outside Seattle, Washington. He had

This student solved a slow-pouring-ketchup problem by inventing a stand that would always keep condiments ready to go.

a system installed that automatically turns on the lights in a room when someone enters it. This allows him to save electricity and lightbulbs. Could you invent a similar system to use at home? You could buy a motion detector and electronic components from an electronics store, and plug household lights into the system. Electronics stores might also have books and experts to help you. Never experiment with electricity without the supervision of a knowledgable adult.

If you like working with electronics, you can imagine lots of other inventions to work on. Chess players need an inexpensive clock for their games. After one person moves, she pushes a switch that turns off her clock and starts her opponent's. Can you make an electronic clock that will keep track of two different times and turn off and on with two switches?

Cleanup. What cleanup jobs do you have at home? How could you make them easier? Someone might have to clean out rain gutters a few times a year. This job can be dangerous to do when perched on a ladder or stooped over at the edge of the roof. Can you make a tool so someone can clean rain gutters while standing on the ground?

At the Store

Grocery bags. People are environmentally conscious these days, and one way to cut down on waste is to reduce the number of disposable bags we use when buying groceries. Some people take cloth bags so they do not have to use the disposable ones the store gives away. But all of these bags present problems: The avocado is smashed into guacamole on the way home as it is squished between the cereal box and the carton of milk. Yuck is everywhere.

How about inventing a new grocery bag that keeps crushable fruits and vegetables separate from the canned and packaged goods? Maybe you could put pockets on the outside where fruits can ride safely and securely. When you put the bags down in the car, how would you make sure the fruits do not get squished or roll out onto the floor?

We recognize that getting the ice cream home before it melts has a high priority. Should your bag have a special insulated section to hold frozen foods?

Maybe it could also have a small pocket where you could stuff your shopping list and the cash register receipt. Maybe another pocket could hold coupons.

Where is the ketchup? While you are thinking about groceries, also think about helping people find those special items they are looking for that could be anywhere in the store. If you like to work with computers, could you figure out a system so shoppers can easily find the locations of those items, rather than searching to ask one of the supermarket employees?

Maybe your system could use voice recognition so shoppers could speak into a microphone to state what they are looking for, and the computer screen would show the item and give the aisle number. Maybe it could also show a map of the store with a big "X" where the desired goodie is shelved.

Grocery carts. Since grocer Sylvan Goldman made the first shopping cart in 1936, millions of carts have carried groceries from the store to the car. The first cart, which was mocked-up with a folding chair, two baskets, and some wheels, has been improved by many inventors over the years. What might you add?

Watch people in the store to see what problems they have. Is it possible for squirming children to fall out of the child seat on the cart? Women would appreciate having a secure place in the cart to stow their pocketbooks. If you made a partial second deck, you could store delicate foods like fresh fruit. Is there an easier way to carry heavy and bulky items like cases of soda or large boxes of detergent?

While thinking about grocery carts, also think about the handbaskets they offer shoppers. Try using one to see how awkward and uncomfortable it can be. What could you make that works better?

Chapter 7

More Things You Can Invent

People are serious about recreation. They spend enormous sums of money on sports equipment, toys, and games. If you create an invention that will help someone ski better, drive a golf ball farther, or make exercising easier, it could become a popular product.

Take a stroll through a toy store or a sporting goods store and look for products that you have never seen before. Some products will offer solutions to problems and others will not solve any problem but will be fun. Check out the display areas near the store entrance and exit. These areas are stocked with inexpensive new products that people may purchase on impulse.

Visiting a store and looking for new things is market research. Conduct some market research in stores to see what ideas you can generate for your inventing.

In Your Car

Snack center. Do you ever get hungry when traveling by car? Would you like to have some food and drinks on hand?

Can you design a snack center for your car? Would it sit on the floor or on the seat? You would want to insulate it so cold drinks stay cold. Would you make slots so you can slide in cans of soda or juice? How about including a container for your favorite chips or cookies? Do you need two containers to accommodate different snacks? Will you want a place to store napkins to clean up greasy fingers?

If you stop at fast-food places and get meals to go, do you have a problem balancing the bag of fries, your burger, and your drink while you open the ketchup packet? What type of lap or seat tray could you make that would hold your food and make it easier to eat?

Backseat fun. Do you ever get bored on long drives? Why not create a game to play in the backseat? You could make a game board out of cloth and use Velcro to hold the game pieces to the board. Players could roll up the game when they are through playing and still have all the pieces in the right places when they start again.

What should be the objective of the game? It could be related to cars, highways, or finding your way to Grandmother's house. Or it could require you to recall license plates or billboard signs.

Car smart. On long car trips, do you take all sorts of stuff like music CDs, books or magazines to read, and games to play on the seat beside you? By the end of the trip, the seat probably looks like a tornado hit it.

What the backseat drivers of the country need is a seat organizer! Make a container that will not slide off the seat and will hold the right amount of stuff to take on a car trip. If you add handles to it, you will be able to haul it out of the car and into your house or motel.

Toys and Games

Since you probably spend a lot of time playing, you are an expert on toys and games. You know what makes a good game or toy, so why not use your expertise to design a new one?

Take a look at all the games and toys you have at home. Could you start with one of those and make changes to improve it? Could you take parts from two or more games and combine them to make something better? Or, could you modify one of them to give it a more modern theme?

Board games. Visit any large toy store and you will find board games. Lots of them! Counting all the different board games at a store should convince you that board games are a big business.

Have you noticed the diversity in board games? Checkers has been popular for many years, and yet it consists solely of a board and identical-shaped pieces painted either red or black. Chess uses the same checkerboard but has six different pieces. Monopoly uses pieces to mark your progress on the board; dice to add the element of chance to the game; cards to add more chance; deeds, houses, and hotels to keep track of ownership of property; and fake money so you can transact business and determine the winner. Checkers, chess, and Monopoly are all popular games, and they range from simple to complex.

In this board game, built from recycled materials, players try to be the first one to get to the top of the pyramid.

Other games test your recall (Trivial Pursuit), dexterity and balance (Jenga), critical thinking (Clue), and vocabulary and spelling (Scrabble). Some depend on luck (Candy Land) and use dice, spinners, or cards.

In this crowded field of games, can you invent a new one? Inventors create new games each year. You are limited only by your imagination in designing a game and your persistence in making it work.

There are several ways to come up with a concept for a game. One is to start with a popular game and change a few elements to create a new game. For example, start with Monopoly, one of the best-selling games of all times. If you like television shows, you could recast Monopoly into a new game based on the entertainment industry. Possibly you would call it "Ratings," and make the object of the game to take your television network to the top of the ratings list. Spaces on the board could be stations you buy, boosting your network's ratings. Cards of chance could bring Hollywood celebrities to your network, or take them away. Your network could negotiate with the Federal Communications Commission to gain more broadcast rights.

To create your own game idea based on Monopoly, list each of the components of Monopoly. These include the board, properties you can buy, money, cards of chance, and dice, to name a few. Now consider how you might change each of these elements to fit a new theme. You may want to add some new components, ones that Monopoly does not have, and not use some of the ones that Monopoly does have. The product has to be fundamentally different from Monopoly or else it will not be a new product. So make lots of changes.

Another approach is to start with an activity that you enjoy and know well. If you like downhill skiing, could you make a game based on skiing? List all the components of skiing—the hill or mountain, the different runs, snow, ski lift, equipment, moguls, dangers (trees, cliffs)—and think how you could incorporate each into a game. Or you could create a knowledge-based game on skiing: Ski-trivia.

If you want to create an educational board game, list the information you want the players to learn during the game. How will you incorporate the information so players will discover it while playing?

Once you have the concept for a game and a few of the rules, move directly into the mock-up stage. Do not worry about the details just yet, as you will change rules and components of the game after you have played it a few times. Get the mock-up developed only to the point that lets you try the game. Then get some friends to play it.

As you play, keep a record of problems that arise and suggestions that players have. You will want to rewrite the rules several times so that they promote fun and fair play. You can record all this information in your inventor's log.

After you have played the game a few times and have ideas on how to improve it, make another mock-up. This time, have people play the game while you watch. Give them a printed copy of the rules. If they have to ask you questions about what the rules mean, you need to rewrite the rules for greater clarity. If they agree that more specific information is needed, ask them for suggestions for an appropriate rule. You can add it to your next mock-up.

When you are satisfied that the game and its rules are working well, collect some data to use in your display. You will want to be able to say how long the game takes to play, how many players can play, what the appropriate age range is, and if materials other than the ones provided with the game are needed. You will want to get data on how people like the game, possibly quotes ("This is the best game . . .") or statistics ("Seven out of ten players liked this game better than . . ."). What kind of questionnaire could you devise that would give you numerical data to use in your display?

For educational games, you will want to see whether the players learned the information you were trying to convey. The best way to measure learning is to give a pretest, then a posttest. Determine what they knew before they played and what they know after having played. These data, shown in a graph, would be a strong addition to your display board.

For a display of your game at an invention contest or fair, you will want to have several things: the best mock-up or prototype available; photographs of people playing the game (see rules of each contest for how to use photographs); quantitative analysis of players' reactions to the game; and information on how you came up with the idea, the objective of the game, and the rules.

To modify the game of chess, you could replace chess pieces with pieces that look like football players. Maybe the pawns are changed to become linemen, crouched down in a three-point stance. Rooks become ends; knights become tackles; and bishops become guards. Maybe the quarterback takes on the power of the queen, and the coach is crowned king.

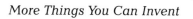

Have friends play your game and record any problems they meet or suggestions they have for it.

Or invent a new game with eleven pieces, but play it like chess on a chessboard.

Spy movies are still popular after all the James Bond and other spy flicks. Could you make a spy game? Would you use a game board like chess and checkers? or one like Monopoly? What kind of cards would you use: chance cards, clue cards, partner cards, or cards giving the hero different vehicles for transportation?

Sure hands. A twelve-year-old boy invented a training aid for basketball. His invention is a handprint that attaches to basketballs to show people how to hold their hands when shooting. The Sporting Goods Manufacturers Association thought it was one of the best new products for 1998.

Starting with the idea of making something to show people where to hold their hands for a game, what other sports can you think of that would benefit from such a device? What activities outside of sports require exact hand placement? What activities require some other placement of hands or feet for safety or ease of operation?

Batter up. It is fun to bat a ball, but not as much fun if you have to chase it to get it back. Invent an automatic retrieval system so players can practice batting without having to run a marathon. Could you attach the ball to a line you anchor in the ground? Maybe use some elastic, but not the kind that will spring the ball right back at you.

Or you could make a home batting cage of mesh or net material. Could a batting cage also have targets for throwing balls? If you invent a system that works for baseball, can you adapt it for golf? What other sports need a cage?

Bowling. On a warm summer evening, lawn bowling would be fun. Invent your own version of the game. Decide what the object of the game is, what balls and other equipment you need, and how you will keep score. Then you will need a specialized bag to carry in all the equipment.

Construction toys. Tinkertoys, Lincoln Logs, Lego toys, and Erector Sets are examples of construction toys. Throughout this century, they have been some of the most popular toys; all the examples (except Lincoln Logs) were among the first toys inducted into the National Toy Hall of Fame.

Can you create a new construction toy? You could use recyclable materials. Would you add pieces so children could make cars and trucks, or just buildings? How would you make your construction set more fun than Lego toys? You might ask

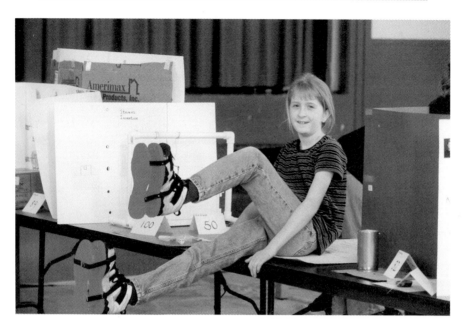

This sports invention helps a basketball player jump higher.

children what they like about building with these types of toys, and see if you can find something that would make the experience better.

Accessories. If you start with the most popular toys today, can you create an accessory for one? For example, if G. I. Joe were popular, could you invent a parachute attachment so he could float to the ground from your second-story window? If all your friends are playing with Lego toys, what do they need? Maybe a specialized box to carry them in, or a "cake box" so they could carry their finished models to show friends, without having the models fall apart.

People who have many electronic games may need some way of neatly storing them so all the game cartridges are in one place. The storage unit might need to include space for different remote controls and their cables. It could also have a score card so you could find out who had the highest score on Tetris or Super Mario Brothers 14.

Young children love to play with model cars, trucks, and airplanes. Provide an accessory for them in the form of a structure for them to play on. You could make a blanket with roads, stores, schools, and homes cut out of different-colored fabrics and sewed or glued on. Or you might make a three-dimensional play structure, like a dollhouse. Could you make a racecourse or ramp so people could race their model cars? For remote-control cars, create an obstacle course with jumps and ramps.

Your Turn to Invent

By now you may have lots of ideas of things you would like to invent, as well as different approaches you may consider to make the invention work. As you write your ideas in your inventor's log, keep adding new ideas to your log and new ways to make your ideas work.

It is time to complete your invention contest project. Steps 4–9 will help you finish your project and enjoy the invention contest.

Chapter 8

Planning Your Invention Contest Project

After you have completed Steps 1–3 that were covered in Chapter 4 and you know what problem you want to solve, you can start planning the project that you will present at the invention contest. Your goal is to assemble the best project to display. Your job will be easier if you create a list of what you will need to do and record it in your inventor's log.

Step 4: Do Your Research

Start to gather information on the problem you are trying to solve. For example, if you were going to invent a better brake for wheelchairs, you would want to know how many people use wheelchairs. You would also want to know about existing brakes and what needs to be improved. There is no sense in inventing a new one if the existing ones work fine.

If you were going to invent a new board game, you could check the reference section of your public library to get information on how many board games exist and how many are sold each year. Companies that make board games could give you information on how many they sell. You could call their public relations department to get information. You might also find information on the Internet.

Before you start digging, make a list of questions that would be interesting to answer. Ask your parents or friends what they would like to know about the type of product you are going to invent, and use those questions to guide your research.

Step 5: Find a Solution

To find a good idea for an invention that solves your problem or improves a product, start with many ideas. Chapter 5 may have helped you get different ideas. Once you have some solid ideas, select the ones that seem most likely to solve the problem. Some ideas might be so complex that you could not build them; skip these and select one that you can make a model of. Once you have made your selection, you can start building.

Step 6: Build a Mock-up

The difference between inventing and thinking of an idea is that in inventing you actually make something. Before you make the actual product, you make a series of models called mock-ups.

Once you have sketched the design you want to use, it is time to make the first mock-up. This might not look much like the final model, or prototype, that you will submit to the contest. The prototype will look just like the completed device if you were to buy it in a store, but the first few mock-ups can be rough drafts.

A mock-up offers several benefits. You can use a mock-up to see where your invention needs improving. It helps you see how different pieces of the invention will work together. You can ask people to try using your mock-up to see whether they like it. And you can take photographs or videos of someone using it, for your competition display.

For your first model, do not invest much time or materials in making it look good. Each time you make a new mock-up you will incorporate improvements, and you might make four or five before deciding you have the design exactly how you want it.

Will you make your mock-ups at full scale? That is, will they be the same size as the invention? For really big inventions, your mock-up might be much smaller, or for tiny devices, you might want a mock-up many times larger. If you were going to invent a new monster truck, your first few mock-ups might be sized to fit on a small table. Having to build a full-scale mock-up of a truck would take too long.

Use mock-ups to test the size and scale of the invention and to see whether the parts fit together. Later versions of the mock-up might be working models that you can test, or even give to others to test. Mock-ups are your way of test-driving your invention before committing to one design.

There is a big difference between having an idea of how to do something and actually making it work, which is the real challenge of inventing. The fun begins when you try to solve any problems that arise as you are designing your invention. You really learn the most at this stage. Inventors are

Mock-ups are a way to test an invention before making a commitment to the final design. This invention is a fire starter for campers.

lifelong learners because each project they tackle forces them to learn something new.

Materials to Use

For your first mock-ups, you will want to use materials that are easy to work with and inexpensive. Cardboard, paper, and wood are good choices. You can find other materials and component parts at thrift stores and garage sales. Do not be concerned with the appearance of your mock-up; just get it together quickly. Why the rush? Because after you build the first mock-up, you will see things you need to change, and you do not want to waste time making a model that you will soon throw away.

Because you want to work quickly, use adhesives to hold the mock-up together. A hot-glue gun is a great tool. Superglues hold well but are expensive and can be messy. You can use glue sticks for holding paper on paper, such as fastening data and graphics to the poster board for your display. Or use tape to hold the components together.

If these materials are not adequate for your mock-up or you do not have the skills to make component parts, search for welding, cabinet, or repair shops that do small jobs. Often you can get parts fabricated for just a few dollars. Look in the telephone directory or ask at hobby stores for the names of people you could hire to do the work. Do not forget to check with friends, neighbors, and relatives who may have fabrication skills and would be delighted to help.

Getting Help

You might find that you run into problems you are unable to solve without outside help. Where do you turn for help?

There are lots of places to try, and no one place is always right for what you need. At a public library you can find some resources. For information on where to buy a part or material, ask the librarian for the *Thomas Register of American Manufacturers*. It lists all the manufacturers in America and the items they make. A second resource is *McRae's Blue Book* that also lists manufacturers.

An engineer, either with a company or at a college, may help, too. He or she can suggest things to try and may know local sources of materials and services. You can also check the telephone directory (Yellow Pages). If you need something welded or made of plastic, you will be able to find local companies that do that kind of work.

The Internet is a great resource for finding companies and for getting questions answered. There is someone in the electronic landscape who can help you; the challenge is for you to locate that person. Ask a parent, teacher, or librarian for help. Use safe communicating skills when corresponding on the Internet. Do not give your home address or phone number, or the school's name.

Inventing clubs are another place to go to find help. There are clubs across America, and many have members with years of experience and eagerness to help. To find clubs, check the listings in Chapter 9, search the Web, or ask local patent attorneys (lawyers who help inventors get patents and defend their legal rights). You can find patent attorneys in the Yellow Pages (under "Attorneys").

You may find help at a technology or business incubator. Incubators are organizations that help inventors and businesspeople start new companies. There are more than two hundred incubators in the United States. They are full of people with creative ideas. Call your city or county government, or local chamber of commerce, to see if they know of a nearby incubator. When you locate one, ask whether you can visit them and talk to inventors and entrepreneurs about your project. You may not find a person with the expertise you are looking for, but you will probably find people who can steer you to the information you need.

Step 7: Test Your Mock-up

Once you have built your mock-up, it is time to see how well it works. An invention needs to be effective, and the only way to know whether it works is to test it.

If you are inventing a game or a garden tool, have people try the mock-up. They will point out design problems you will want to change. After people test your mock-up, you can build an improved mock-up and ask them to test it again. Keep going until the testers agree that it works really well.

When your mock-up is ready, test it once more with a new group of people. You will want to devise a test that yields numeric data, so you can represent it in a graph. For a new garden shovel, you might measure how much dirt it picks up compared with a standard shovel. For a board game, you might measure how often people play it or how they rate it on a scale of one to ten.

You will want to plan the testing carefully, because judges will look closely at the testing data and your analysis. If you

It is a good idea to have different groups of people test your mock-up.

can show that your invention works, that it solves the problem you set out to solve, and that it solves the problem better than other approaches, you will have a winning entry and possibly a new product. Remember to keep records of your tests and the data you collected in your inventor's log.

How will you demonstrate that your invention does what you say it does? Photographs of people using your invention tell the story. You do not need lots of photographs, but a few (five or six) can show the judges how it works. You could also include a photo of yourself (if not prohibited by the rules) building the mock-up.

Graphs of data help convince even skeptics. You can say that your invention will solve a problem, but if you supply data from tests, you will prove your point. Graphs are the best way to show the data. Ideally you will be able to show how much better your invention works than existing devices or methods. If you cannot measure the effectiveness directly, you can have people give numeric ratings to your invention and to existing devices. Then you can compare the ratings.

If you designed a new puzzle that was fun but really hard, you might show how long people spent putting it together. You could time people playing with it for the first time and compare those times with how long they played with similar games already in stores. Compute the average times played for each and make a bar chart, with the idea that the longer they played with a puzzle, the more challenging and better it actually is. Or you could ask them to rate the puzzle (on how much fun or how challenging it was to solve) compared with other puzzles.

If you are not familiar with data collection, analysis, and graphing, get some help at school. Ask a teacher in math or science to help you design experiments to test your invention.

Although your goal in testing is to show how great your invention is, do not lose sight of your integrity. That is, do not "fake the data." You can always overcome a few flaws in your invention, but you cannot regain the trust of others once it is lost. It is better to be painfully honest and admit that your invention is not perfect, than to suggest it is better than it really is.

Step 8: Make a Prototype

It is difficult for people to look at a roughly made mock-up and envision what the product will do and what it will look like. The prototype solves this problem.

A prototype is a mock-up that looks and operates like the product. The model you show at an invention contest should be a prototype; it is what judges will want to see. If possible, rig it up so it operates for them. If you cannot, use video or still photographs to show it in operation.

A prototype should pass the retail test: Does it work well enough and look good enough for someone to purchase it at a store? If it does, you are ready for the invention contest.

Making the prototype can be difficult. Getting something made of plastic may not be possible. You may need to make two prototypes: One that looks like the product and one that works like the product. You could make one prototype out of wood or other materials and paint it to look the way you imagine the product would look. The second prototype, made of Lego toys or other construction toys, could demonstrate the operation of your invention.

Step 9: Create a Display

Imagine you are judging the invention contest. There are rows after rows of tables filled with things young people have invented. You do not have time to examine each display closely, but you have to pick a few for awards. How will you do it?

As a judge, you would probably scan the entries and spend more time on the ones that caught your attention. An attractive display board with color photographs and neat text might warrant closer inspection. An interesting-looking and neatly constructed prototype would capture your eye. Graphs of test results would give the impression immediately that the inventor had tested his or her invention. In a few minutes you might identify which entries you would consider for prizes.

Form a mental picture of what a wonderful display looks like, and then create it. First, check the contest rules to see whether they specify the size available for each display. Then decide what material you will use for the display panel: foam board, wood, or cardboard. Foam board (there are several brand names) is probably the best material. You can find it at art, hobby, and some office supply stores.

Make a sketch of where the information will go on the board. Again check the contest rules to see whether they have a preferred or required format. You will want the name of your invention in letters large enough to read at a distance of at least ten feet. You will want all the lettering to be crisp, neat, and legible. Use as few words as possible and rely more on pictures, graphs, and other illustrations. When possible, print the text and graphs you will use on a quality computer printer. If you do not have one at home, see whether there is one you can use at school or at your public library.

When all the components are ready to be attached to the board, first lay them in position so you can check spacing and sequencing. The board should present a story starting with the problem you selected and ending with the solution—your invention. Have someone else look at your laid-out board and give you suggestions. Only when you are convinced that everything is where it should be do you bring out the glue and attach the components.

You could present detailed information either in your inventor's log or in a loose-leaf notebook. Place either of these on the table in front of your display board. Mark the cover in stand-out lettering with the name of the project. Also make sure that your name and address are written on the inside front cover.

You should display your prototype. If it can operate so judges can try it, that is even better. If you had a succession of mock-ups, you might show a few of them or pictures of them.

You may be required to show an approved entry form or project number as part of your display. If the judges cannot find your number, they may not be able to record their observations about your project.

Step Back

When your display is set up for the invention contest, take a minute to step back and appreciate the product. You will have worked hard to get to this point, so give yourself a pat on the back. Whether or not you win a prize, you have become an

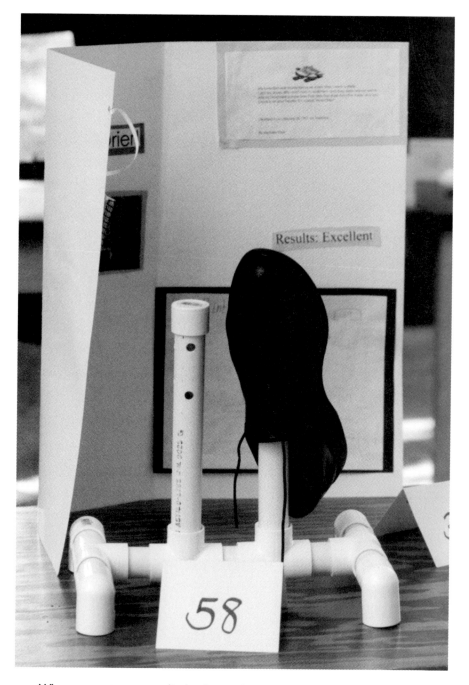

When you set up your display for an invention contest, make sure your approved entry form or project number is visible to the judges. In wet climates, this shoe dryer could be a popular product.

inventor and learned lots of new skills you will be able to use later. Congratulations!

Tips for the Contest

You do not have to win a prize to be a winner. However, your goal at the outset is to win the invention contest. Give it your best effort. Here are some suggestions to help you make your project the best it can be.

- Invention contests have criteria for the judges to follow when evaluating projects. You have the best chance of winning if you keep these criteria in mind during your invention process. If the contest information does not include the criteria, ask for a copy. Write the criteria in your inventor's log and refer to them often.

- See what inventions won in previous years. If the rules have not changed since then, last year's winners might indicate the type of projects the judges will be looking for again. Also, you may be able to talk to one of the judges before the contest. See if you can get the judge's perspective on what a good entry should be.

- Have enough area for your prototype to work. Practice demonstrating the prototype operation before the contest so that you will feel comfortable on contest day with the judges.

- Test data can be a powerful endorsement. If you have data to show that your invention solves a problem faster, easier, or better than an existing solution, highlight the data in graphical form. Ask a math or science teacher to help you display the data so it shows the advantages of your invention.

- Be familiar with your test data and make sure the graphs and tables are clearly presented. Be ready to explain your results to the judges.

- Testing can also include gathering quotes from people who have used your invention. Provide a snapshot of their testing it and a short quote from them on how it works. The more prominent the tester is, the more the judges will be influenced. Could you get the mayor to test your new throwing toy?

- You might include your initial sketches and various mock-ups to show how your thinking progressed throughout the project. Your inventor's log would show the judges the work you put in.

Criteria for Judging

One invention contest uses the following grading scale for evaluating contest entries. Judges can award up to 100 points as follows:

25 points for the greatest potential benefit to society

25 points for the most innovative invention

25 points for the best-performing prototype

15 points for the effectiveness of the display

10 points for the design and neatness of the display

For each of these criteria, judges can award from zero up to the maximum number of points listed. Even though these criteria focus less on the display than on the other qualities of your work, judges will form immediate opinions on the quality of your project just by looking at the display.

Since the responsibility of the judges is to find a small number of projects to honor, their job is to eliminate most of the projects from consideration. To keep in the running, you must have a neat and attractive display, as well as a good invention.

You may read the judging criteria and interpret them differently than someone else may. Ask two or more adults to read the criteria for the contest and then look at your project and display. Have them point out where your project may be improved. Listen to their comments and see if you can find ways to make your project even better.

Chapter 9

Invention Programs and Organizations

You can find educational programs and people with expertise in inventing to help you develop your creativity and inventing potential. Typically, however, they are not easy to find. A good place to start inquiring is with teachers at your school. They may know of existing programs or be interested in starting some. If your teachers do not know about any programs, the following learning programs and inventors organizations may help you get started.

Learning Programs

Camp Invention. Inventure Place, home of the National Inventors Hall of Fame, coordinates Camp Invention programs in many states. The one-week camps encourage elementary school children to be creative and inventive. To find a camp near you or to organize one at your school, contact:

Camp Invention
Inventure Place
221 South Broadway Street
Akron, OH 44308-1505
Telephone: (800) 968-4332
Fax: (330) 762-6313
Web site: http://www.invent.org

Kids Invent Toys. California State University, Fresno, offers this program at sites throughout the United States and in foreign countries to help elementary and secondary school students learn how to invent and start their own businesses. It is a weeklong camp in which students make a variety of toys as they develop their own ideas for toy inventions. By the end of the week, student teams will have invented a toy, created a Web page to promote it, and learned how to start their own toy-making business. For more information, contact them at:

Institute for Developing Entrepreneurial Action (IDEA)
Sid Craig School of Business
5245 N. Backer Avenue
California State University, Fresno
Fresno, CA 93740-0007
Telephone: (209) 278-2326
Fax: (209) 278-4911
Web site: http://www.craig.csufresno.edu/fac/
   STEARNS/ENTRHOME.HTM

National Collegiate Inventors and Innovators Alliance. This organization awards grants to colleges to "nurture invention, innovation, and entrepreneurship." The colleges can offer programs for precollege students. For information on current programs, contact them at:

National Collegiate Inventors and Innovators Alliance (NCIIA)

Hampshire College—LM
Amherst, MA 01002-5001
Telephone: (413) 559-5309
College Web site: http://www.hampshire.edu

Odyssey of the Mind (OM). OM is a worldwide program to foster creative thinking. OM teams design solutions to long-term problems and demonstrate their solutions in performances lasting eight minutes. They also compete in creative-thinking contests. OM organizes training camps in the summer months around the country. For more information about OM programs in your state, contact them at:

OM Association, Inc.

P.O. Box 547
Glassboro, NJ 08028
Telephone: (609) 881-1603
Fax: (609) 881-3596
Web site: http://www.odysseyofthemind.com

Women Inventors Project. This is a nonprofit organization formed "to increase the number of successful women inventors and entrepreneurs in Canada." They offer a curriculum for "An Invention Workshop for Girls" and other materials. Contact them at:

Women Inventors Project

1 Greensboro Drive, Suite 302
Etobicoke, Ontario
Canada, M9W 1C8

Inventors Organizations

Inventors clubs exist to help members develop their ideas into inventions. Try contacting local inventors groups, from the list below, to see whether they have regular meetings you could attend. If you do not find a group near you, check with local patent attorneys (see the telephone directory) to see whether they know of any groups of inventors. You can also contact the national organizations to see whether there are any groups forming.

National organizations:	**Inventors Clubs of America, Inc.** P.O. Box 450261 Atlanta, GA 31145-0261 Telephone: (404) 816-4774 Fax: (404) 846-0982
	Inventors Workshop International 3537 Old Conejo Road, Suite 120 Newbury Park, CA 91320 Telephone: (805) 962-5722

Organizations by state[1]:	
Alabama:	**Alabama Inventors Association** 3409 Fountain Circle Montgomery, AL 36116
Arkansas:	**Arkansas Inventors Congress** One State Capital Mall Little Rock, AR 72201
California:	**California Inventors Council** P.O. Box 2036 Sunnyvale, CA 94087

California:	**Inventors of California** 215 Rheem Boulevard Moraga, CA 94556
	Inventors Council of California 250 Vernon Street Oakland, CA 94610
	Inventors Resource Center P.O. Box 5105 Berkeley, CA 94705
	National Congress of Inventors Organizations 215 Rheem Boulevard Moraga, CA 94556
	National Inventors Foundation 345 West Cypress Street Glendale, CA 91204
	Technology Transfer Society 11720 West Pico Boulevard Los Angeles, CA 90064
Colorado:	**Affiliated Inventors Foundation** 501 Iowa Avenue Colorado Springs, CO 80909
	National Inventors Cooperative Association P.O. Box 6585 Denver, CO 80206
Florida:	**Central Florida Inventors Club** 4849 Victory Drive Orlando, FL 32808

Florida:	**The Inventors Club** Route 11, P.O. Box 379 Pensacola, FL 32514
	Palm Beach Society of American Inventors P.O. Box 26 Palm Beach, FL 33480
	Society of American Inventors 505 East Jackson Street, Suite 204 Tampa, FL 33602
	Society for Inventors and Entrepreneurs 306 Georgetown Drive Casselberry, FL 32707
	Tampa Bay Inventor's Council 805 West 118 Street Tampa, FL 33612
Georgia:	**Inventor Associates of Georgia** 637 Linwood Avenue NE Atlanta, GA 30306
	Inventors Association of Georgia 241 Freyer Drive NE Marietta, GA 30060
Hawaii:	**Inventors Council of Hawaii** P.O. Box 27844 Honolulu, HI 96827
Illinois:	**Chicago High Tech Association** 20 North Wacker Drive, Suite 1929 Chicago, IL 60606

Illinois:	**Inventors Council of Chicago** 53 West Jackson Boulevard, Suite 1041 Chicago, IL 60604
Indiana:	**Indiana Inventors Association** 612 Ironwood Drive Plainfield, IN 46168
	International Association of Professional Inventors Route 1, Box 1074 Shirley, IN 47384
	Inventors and Entrepreneurs Society P.O. Box 2224 Hammond, IN 46323
Massachusetts:	**Innovation Invention Network** 132 Sterling Street West Boylston, MA 01583
	Inventors Association of New England P.O. Box 325 Lexington, MA 02173
Michigan:	**Inventors Council of Michigan** 2200 Bonisteel Boulevard Ann Arbor, MI 48109
Minnesota:	**Inventors and Technology Transfer Society** P.O. Box 14775 Minneapolis, MN 55414
	Midwest Inventors Society P.O. Box 335 Saint Cloud, MN 56301

Minnesota:	**Minnesota Inventors Congress** P.O. Box 71 Redwood Falls, MN 56283
	Society of Minnesota Inventors 20231 Basalt Street NW Anoka, MN 55303
Mississippi:	**Confederacy of Mississippi Inventors** 4759 Nailor Road Vicksburg, MS 39180
	Mississippi Inventors Workshop 4729 Kings Highway Jackson, MS 39206
	Mississippi Society of Scientists and Inventors P.O. Box 2244 Jackson, MS 39205
Missouri:	**Inventors Association of St. Louis** P.O. Box 16544 Saint Louis, MO 63105
Nebraska:	**Kearney Inventors Association** 2001 Avenue A, P.O. Box 607 Kearney, NB 68847
	Lincoln Inventors Association P.O. Box 94666 Lincoln, NB 68509
	Omaha Inventors Club 11145 Mill Valley Road Omaha, NB 68145

New Jersey:	**American Society of Inventors** 402 Cynwyd Drive Absecon, NJ 08201
	National Society of Inventors 539 Laurel Place South Orange, NJ 07079
New York:	**Society of Professional Inventors** SUNY Farmingdale, Lupton Hall Farmingdale, NY 11735
Ohio:	**Columbus Inventors Association** 2480 East Avenue Columbus, OH 43202
	Inventors Club of Cincinnati 18 Gambier Circle Cincinnati, OH 45218
	Inventors Council of Dayton 140 E. Monument Avenue Dayton, OH 45402
Oklahoma:	**Invention Development Society** 8502A SW Eighth Street Oklahoma City, OK 73128
	Oklahoma Inventors Congress P.O. Box 75635 Oklahoma City, OK 73147
Oregon:	**Western Inventors Council** P.O. Box 3288 Eugene, OR 97403
Pennsylvania:	**American Society of Inventors** P.O. Box 58426 Philadelphia, PA 19102

Tennessee:	**Appalachian Inventors Group** P.O. Box 388 Oak Ridge, TN 37830
	Tennessee Inventors Association P.O. Box 11225 Knoxville, TN 37939
	Tennessee Inventors Association 1116 Weisgarber Knoxville, TN 37919
Texas:	**Texas Inventors Association** 4000 Rock Creek Drive, Suite 100 Dallas, TX 75204
Utah:	**Intermountain Society of Inventors and Designers** P.O. Box 1056 Tooele, UT 84074
Washington:	**Inventors Association of Washington** P.O. Box 1725 Bellevue, WA 98009
	Northwest Inventors Association 723 East Highland Drive Arlington, WA 98223
Wisconsin:	**Midwest Inventors Group** P.O. Box 1 Chippewa Falls, WI 54729

[1] *Inventors Clubs and Organizations*, n.d. <www.isd.net/abarbeau/consortium/ local.htm> (February 23, 1999).

Chapter 10

After the Invention Contest

Now that you have become an inventor, why stop? If you enjoyed working on your project, keep improving it. You might want to enter next year's contest. Or you might consider transforming your invention into a marketable product. Even if your first invention does not succeed (Edison's first invention, an electric vote counter, worked well but was unsuccessful in the market), you have learned what you need to know to make your next invention a contest winner or a hit in the stores.

You can find Post-it notes, those little yellow tablets of paper with stickum on the back, in most offices across the country. But when Art Fry invented them, no one could see a use for them. Monopoly is the best-selling game of the century, but no company wanted to market it when Charles Darrow first offered it for sale in 1934.

Many people, invention contest judges included, cannot always imagine how new ideas will work. Do not give up on your idea even if the judges did not get excited about it. Ask for their thoughts on your project, and use their analysis to make your project better.

Protecting Your Invention

Getting a patent may be the first thing that comes to mind when thinking about inventions, but you may not need one. Patents are expensive (costing thousands of dollars) and make sense only if you have a solid business plan that indicates your invention will be financially possible to produce. So before rushing out to apply for a patent, do some market research. That is, try to figure out who will buy your product and how much money it will cost to make and sell your invention.

If you decide that the expense of getting a patent is justified by the market potential, ask your parent or teacher to help you contact a patent attorney. Although you can get a

Speak with the judges about your project, and use their suggestions to make your invention better.

patent yourself (see the books listed in the "Further Reading" section at the back of this book), it is not easy. Most people hire a patent attorney. You can find them listed in the telephone directory (Yellow Pages) under the heading "Attorneys."

A patent is a right granted by the federal government. The right excludes other people from copying your invention and making, using, or selling it for a period of time, usually a maximum of seventeen years. That means that you could sue anyone who copies your patent from the time the Patent and Trademark Office (PTO) grants it to you until it expires. The catch is that you have to sue; the government will not prosecute anyone who copies your patent—you have to.

The PTO publishes a brochure called "Basic Facts about Patents" that gives a good overview. To get a copy, write to the Commissioner of Patents and Trademarks, Washington, DC, 20231.

You can also get information on patents by logging on to the Patent and Trademark Office's World Wide Web page. The PTO will send you a copy of a patent for a modest fee. (Want to see the Wright brothers' patent? or the most valuable patent, Alexander Graham Bell's telephone patent? You can get copies mailed to you from the PTO.) If you want more information, contact the office at:

Patent and Trademark Office
Patent Assistance Center
Telephone: (800) PTO-9199 or
(703) 308-HELP
Fax: (703) 305-7786
Web site: http://www.uspto.gov

Or check the patents listed at the Web site:

http://www.patents.ibm.com

Whenever you find a new product, turn it over to look for a patent number, or look on the package it came in. The PTO issues patents sequentially. The first patent was signed by George Washington and Thomas Jefferson (for a process of making potash, which became an important industry in the early years of this country). Patent number 5,000,000 was issued in March 1991 (for a genetically engineered bacterium that recycles waste into fuel), and at the rate Americans are inventing (about 150,000 patents are issued each year), patent number 6,000,000 will be issued near the end of the 1990s. Remembering these dates lets you estimate in what year a recent patent was issued. Of course, the inventor came up with the idea long before the patent was issued. It takes about eighteen months to receive a patent from the time an inventor applies for it.

On some devices you may find the words "Patent Pending." This means that a patent has been applied for, but not yet received. "Patent Pending" carries no legal protection.

Another way to protect your invention is by keeping the technical details secret. If others are not likely to figure out how you made it, why patent it? Coca-Cola is the best example. The process for making it was invented a century ago, but never patented. If it had been patented, imitators could have copied it (after the patent had expired) and sold their same-tasting product in competition with Coke. For Coke, keeping the formula a trade secret was the right choice.

Selling Your Invention

Participating in an invention contest may be your only goal when you start inventing, but you can also aspire to selling

Competing in an invention contest may have been your only goal when you created your device, but you can also sell your invention. This "coneapult" was invented for tossing pine cones as part of a game.

your invention. You could make and sell the product yourself, or sell your invention to a company that already sells similar products, or find a company to make the product for you to sell. You can find information about companies that might buy your invention, or help you make it or sell it, at your library.

Some companies specialize in helping inventors develop their ideas into products. You can find listings of these companies in the telephone Yellow Pages directory under "Product Development." Unfortunately, there are too many such companies that require you to pay fees up front and then do not provide useful services. Before dealing with any company, request a list of customers you can contact for references.

If you take all the information about your invention—including how you are protecting it, how you are going to make it and sell it, along with financial projections—and compile it neatly into a document, you will have a business plan. Business leaders will ask to see your business plan before they commit to investing their resources in your invention.

Taking the Product to Market

By now you have learned that inventing is not just having good ideas, but also transforming them into products and selling them. As hard as it is to come up with a great idea, it is equally hard to make it work, make a salable product, and find business partners. Remember, inventors do not give up.

Further Reading

Caney, Steven. *Steven Caney's Invention Book.* New York: Workman Publishing Company, Inc., 1985.

Carrow, Robert. *Put a Fan in Your Hat!: Inventions, Contraptions & Gadgets Kids Can Build.* New York: McGraw-Hill, 1996.

Flatow, Ira. *They All Laughed . . . From Lightbulbs to Lasers: The Fascinating Stories Behind the Great Inventions That Have Changed Our Lives.* New York: HarperPerennial Publishers, Inc., 1993.

Inventive Genius. Alexandria, Va.: Time-Life, Inc., 1990.

Macaulay, David. *The New Way Things Work.* New York: Houghton Mifflin Company, 1998.

Pressman, David. *Patent It Yourself.* Berkeley, Calif.: Nolo Press, 1997.

Sobey, Ed. *Inventing Stuff.* Palo Alto, Calif.: Dale Seymour Publications, 1996.

Index